For my father (1904–1960)

Draw Me a Star

Eric Carle Draw Me a Star

PAPERSTAR

Penguin Putnam Books for Young Readers

Draw me a star.

And the artist drew a star.

It was a good star.

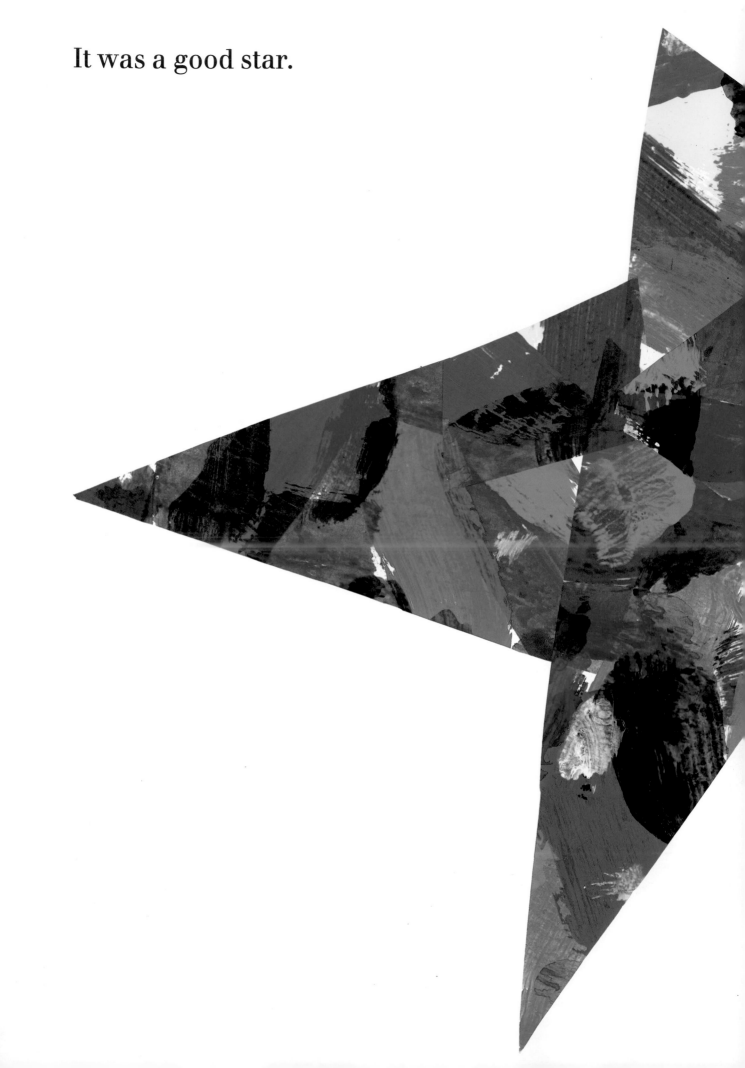

Draw me the sun, said the star.
And the artist drew the sun.
It was a warm sun.

Draw me a tree, said the sun.
And the artist drew a tree.
It was a lovely tree.
Draw me a woman and a man.
And the artist drew a handsome couple.

Draw us a house, said the couple.
And the artist drew a house.
It was a strong house.

Draw me a dog, said the house.
And the artist drew a dog.
It was a big dog.

Draw me a cat, said the dog.
Draw me a bird, said the cat.
Draw me a butterfly, said the bird.

Draw me a flower, said the butterfly.
And the artist drew red and yellow
and blue and purple flowers.

Draw us a cloud, said the flowers.
And the artist drew clouds heavy with rain.

Draw me the night, said the rainbow.
And the artist drew a dark night.

Draw me the moon, said the night.
And the artist drew a full moon.
Draw me a star, said the moon.

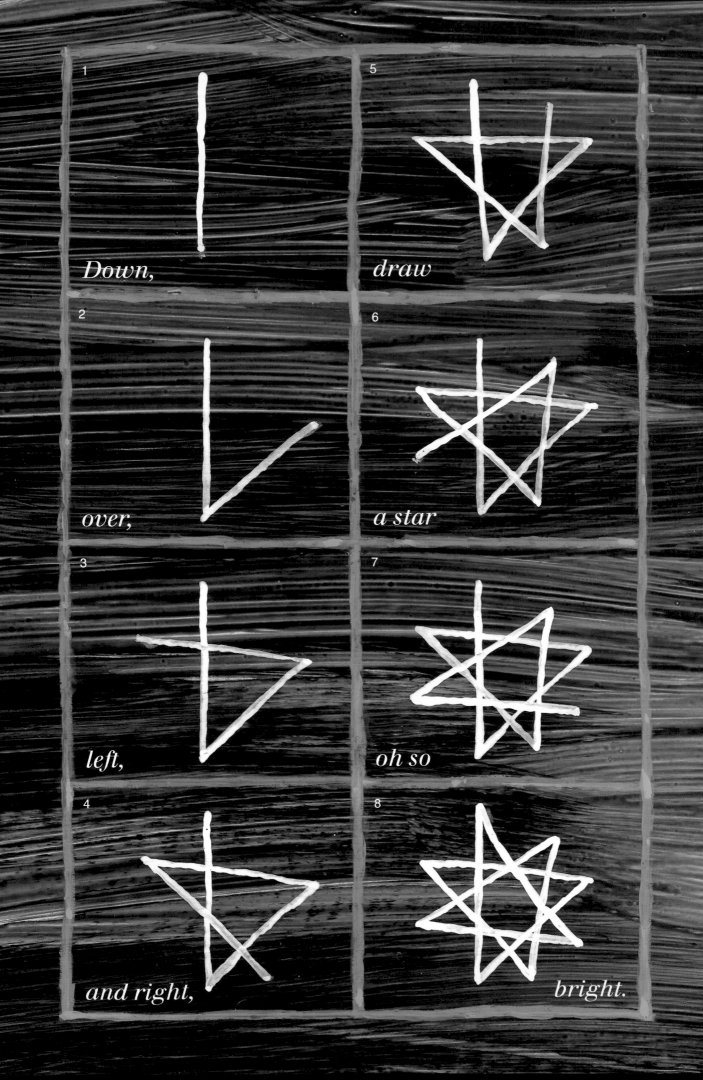

1 Down,

2 over,

3 left,

4 and right,

5 draw

6 a star

7 oh so

8 bright.

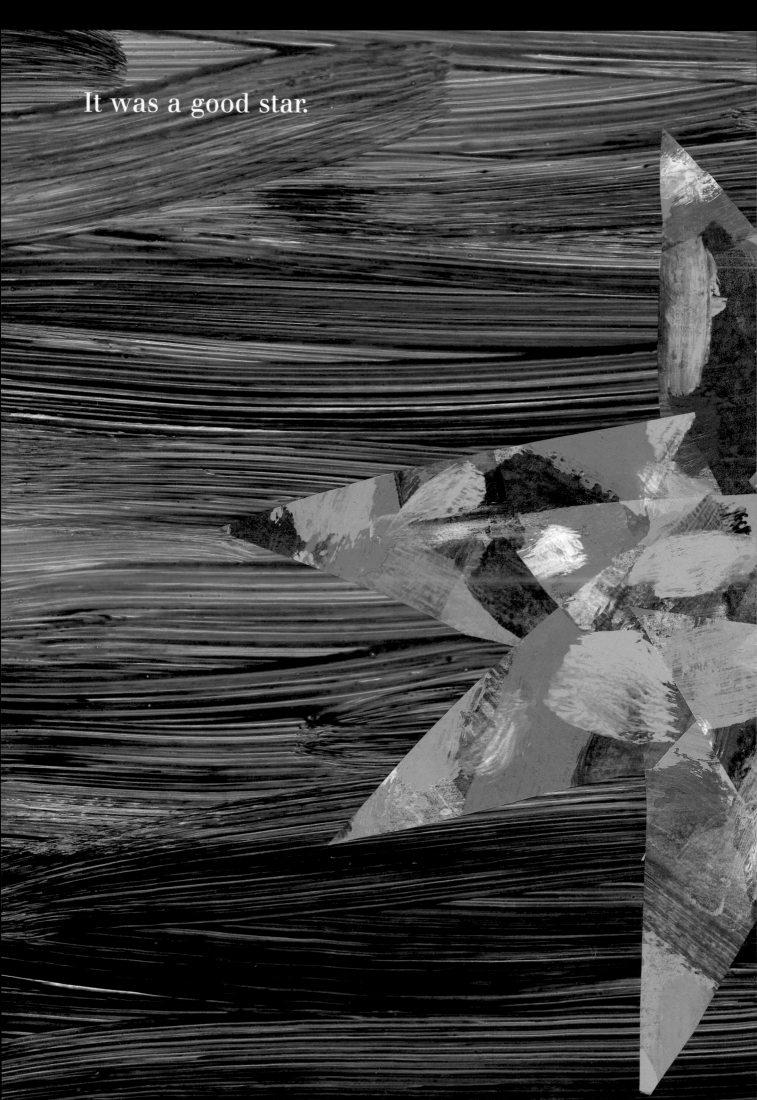

It was a good star.

Hold on to me, said the star to the artist.

Then, together, they traveled across the night sky.

Dear Friends,

When I was a young child my German Oma (Grandmother) scribbled a star for me as she recited this nonsense poem:

KRI KRA KROTEN- FUSS, GÄNSE LAUFEN BAR- FUSS
(KRI KRA TOAD'S FOOT, GEESE WALK BARE- FOOT)

Then last summer on my vacation, I dreamed about shooting stars. The first stars fell into the valleys of the distant hills. More stars fell closer and closer. Finally, a very bright star fell directly on me, not hurting me at all; in fact, it felt pleasant, kind of tingly. After that the star and I rose up and traveled across the night sky.

I had a beginning for a book, and an ending. The middle was easy!

Sincerely,

Eric Carle prepares his own colored tissue papers. Different textures are achieved by using various brushes
to splash, spatter, and fingerpaint acrylic paints onto thin tissue papers. These colored tissue papers then become his palette.
They are cut or torn into shapes as needed and are glued onto white illustration board. Some areas of his designs,
however, are painted directly on the board before the bits of tissue paper are applied to make the collage illustrations.
The art is then scanned by laser and separated into four colors for reproduction on sheetfed offset printing presses.

Library of Congress Cataloging-in-Publication Data
Carle, Eric. Draw me a star / written and illustrated by Eric Carle. p. cm.
Summary: An artist's drawing of a star begins the creation of an entire universe
around him as each successive pictured object requests that he draw more.
[1. Artists—Fiction. 2. Drawing—Fiction.] I. Title. PZ7.C21476Dr 1992 [E]—dc20
91-29055 CIP AC ISBN 0-698-11632-1
9 10 8